MW00964831

SandCastle™

Synonyms

Ella Is Right, Smart and Bright!

Tracy Kompelien

Consulting Editor, Diane Craig, M.A./Reading Specialist

ABDO
Publishing Company

Published by ABDO Publishing Company, 4940 Viking Drive, Edina, Minnesota 55435.
Copyright © 2007 by Abdo Consulting Group, Inc. International copyrights reserved in all countries.
No part of this book may be reproduced in any form without written permission from the publisher.
SandCastle™ is a trademark and logo of ABDO Publishing Company.

Printed in the United States.

Credits
Edited by: Pam Price
Curriculum Coordinator: Nancy Tuminelly
Cover and Interior Design and Production: Mighty Media
Photo Credits: Comstock, Shutterstock, Steve Wewerka

Library of Congress Cataloging-in-Publication Data
Kompelien, Tracy, 1975-
  Ella is right, smart and bright! / Tracy Kompelien.
     p. cm. -- (Synonyms)
  ISBN-13: 978-1-59928-729-4
  ISBN-10: 1-59928-729-3
  1. English language--Synonyms and antonyms--Juvenile literature. I. Title.

PE1591.K647 2007
428.1--dc22
                            2006031427

SandCastle™ books are created by a professional team of educators, reading specialists, and content developers around five essential components—phonemic awareness, phonics, vocabulary, text comprehension, and fluency—to assist young readers as they develop reading skills and strategies and increase their general knowledge. All books are written, reviewed, and leveled for guided reading, early reading intervention, and Accelerated Reader® programs for use in shared, guided, and independent reading and writing activities to support a balanced approach to literacy instruction.

Let Us Know

SandCastle would like to hear your stories about reading this book. What is your favorite page? Was there something hard that you needed help with? Share the ups and downs of learning to read. We want to hear from you! To get posted on the ABDO Publishing Company Web site, send us e-mail at:
sandcastle@abdopublishing.com

SandCastle Level: Fluent

A synonym is a word that has the same or a similar meaning as another word.

Here is a good way to remember what a synonym is:

synonym
=
same
=
similar

3

4

The police officer is polite.

considerate

nice

respectful

cooperative

courteous

well mannered

synonyms

My cousin Joe is young.

small   little

childlike   childish

synonyms

My sister Julie is sometimes mean.

uncaring   hostile   unkind

cruel

nasty   disagreeable

synonyms

Taylor is funny.

humorous

comical   witty

amusing   hilarious

synonyms

My instructor is smart.

sharp

intelligent

bright

knowledgeable

quick

clever

wise

synonyms

Kevin is cooperative. He works well with other kids. His friends like him because he is respectful and fun. Kevin is active but well mannered.

Can you find any synonyms for the word cooperative in the paragraph above?

15

16

synonyms

Sarah is witty. Her jokes are humorous and amusing. She tells stories that are hilarious. Sarah makes people laugh.

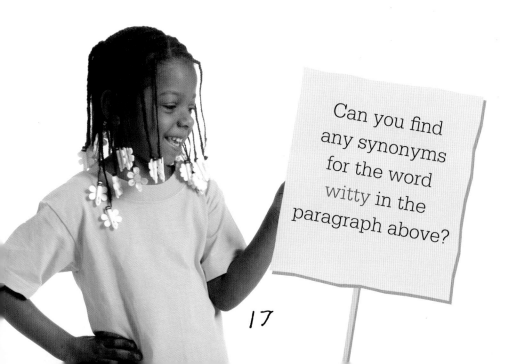

Can you find any synonyms for the word witty in the paragraph above?

17

synonyms

Mrs. Smith is bright. She teaches her class about science. Her lessons are fun and interesting. Mrs. Smith is very knowledgeable.

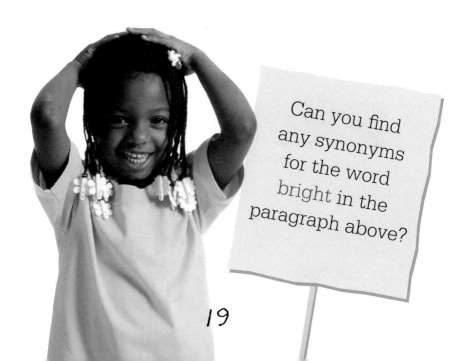

Can you find any synonyms for the word bright in the paragraph above?

What synonyms can you use to describe this amusing clown?

Glossary

cooperative – being willing and able to work with others.

courteous – having good manners.

hilarious – very funny.

hostile – having angry feelings or behavior toward another.

intelligent – having the ability to acquire and use knowledge.

knowledgeable – having or showing knowledge or intelligence.

Words I Know

Nouns

A noun is a person, place, or thing.

class, 19

clown, 20

cousin, 7

friends, 15

instructor, 13

jokes, 17

kids, 15

lessons, 19

people, 17

police officer, 5

science, 19

sister, 9

stories, 17

synonyms, 20

Proper Nouns

A proper noun is the name of a person, place, or thing.

Joe, 7

Julie, 9

Kevin, 15

Mrs. Smith, 19

Sarah, 17

Taylor, 11

Verbs

A verb is an action or being word.

are, 17, 19

can, 20

describe, 20

is, 5, 7, 9, 11, 13, 15, 17, 19

laugh, 17

like, 15

makes, 17

teaches, 19

tells, 17

use, 20

works, 15

Words I Know

Adjectives
An adjective describes something.

active, 15
amusing, 11, 17, 20
bright, 13, 19
childish, 7
childlike, 7
clever, 13
comical, 11
considerate, 5
cooperative, 5, 15
courteous, 5
cruel, 9
disagreeable, 9
fun, 15, 19
funny, 11
her, 17, 19
hilarious, 11, 17

his, 15
hostile, 9
humorous, 11, 17
intelligent, 13
interesting, 19
knowledgeable,
  13, 19
little, 7
mean, 9
my, 7, 9, 13
nasty, 9
nice, 5
other, 15
polite, 5
quick, 13
respectful, 5, 15

sharp, 13
small, 7
smart, 13
this, 20
uncaring, 9
unkind, 9
well, 15
well mannered,
  5, 15
what, 20
wise, 13
witty, 11, 17
young, 7

About SandCastle™

A professional team of educators, reading specialists, and content developers created the SandCastle™ series to support young readers as they develop reading skills and strategies and increase their general knowledge. The SandCastle™ series has four levels that correspond to early literacy development in young children. The levels are provided to help teachers and parents select the appropriate books for young readers.

Emerging Readers
(no flags)

Beginning Readers
(1 flag)

Transitional Readers
(2 flags)

Fluent Readers
(3 flags)

These levels are meant only as a guide. All levels are subject to change.

To see a complete list of SandCastle™ books and other nonfiction titles from ABDO Publishing Company, visit www.abdopublishing.com or contact us at:
4940 Viking Drive, Edina, Minnesota 55435 • 1-800-800-1312 • fax: 1-952-831-1632